The Government of New York

James Bernard

New York

Published in 2015 by The Rosen Publishing Group, Inc.
29 East 21st Street, New York, NY 10010

Book Design: Chris Brand

Photo Credits: Cover, p. 5 © Superstock; p. 7 by Jessica Livingston; pp. 9, 11 Stock Montage/Archive Photos/Getty Images; p. 13 (inset) © Lee Snider/Corbis; p. 13 © Jon Hicks/Corbis; p. 15 (inset) © New York State Office of General Services; p. 15 Ritu Manoj Jethani/Shutterstock.com; p. 17 © Shutterstock.com; p. 19 © TimePix; p. 21 (inset) © Corbis; p. 21 © Lake County Museum/Corbis.

Library of Congress Cataloging-in-Publication Data

Bernard, James.
The government of New York / by James Bernard.
p. cm. — (Spotlight on New York)
Includes index.
ISBN 978-1-4777-7336-9 (pbk.)
ISBN 978-1-4777-7287-4 (6-pack)
ISBN 978-1-4777-7325-3 (library binding)
1. New York (State) — Politics and government — Juvenile literature. I. Bernard, James. II. Title.
JK3416.B47 2015
320.4747—d23

Manufactured in the United States of America

CPSIA Compliance Information: Batch #WS15RC: For further information contact Rosen Publishing, New York, New York at 1-800-237-9932.

Contents

The History of Government in New York State

Government in New York State has grown and changed over the centuries. Before the first Europeans arrived, New York was home to many Native Americans. Different groups of Algonquians lived in the Hudson River valley, on Long Island, and around Manhattan and New Jersey. The five tribes of the Iroquois stretched from Albany to Buffalo. The Iroquois and the Algonquians each had their own forms of government.

In 1624, the Dutch **settled** different communities in what they called New Netherland. These communities had forms of government similar to those used by the Dutch in Europe. When the English took control from the Dutch in 1664, they brought forms of government and laws that they were familiar with in England.

In 1776, **representatives** from thirteen of Britain's North American **colonies** signed the Declaration of Independence. This document declared the colonies free from England. After the colonists won their freedom in the **American Revolution**, they created a **republic**, a form of government where **citizens** elect representatives who make the laws.

The Declaration of Independence was approved in Philadelphia, Pennsylvania, on July 4, 1776. New York's leaders approved it five days later. In this painting, Thomas Jefferson, Benjamin Franklin, and others are shown signing the Declaration of Independence on August 2, 1776. The painting can be seen in the U.S. Capitol Building in Washington, D.C.

Native American Forms of Government

The Algonquians of the Atlantic coast were the first native peoples to encounter European explorers and settlers. New York State was home to many different groups of Algonquians, including the Mahicans, Canarsees, Wappingers, and others. Each Algonquian tribe had its own form of government. Most tribes had some form of tribal council. The members of the council varied from tribe to tribe. Tribal councils were usually led by a chief.

The Iroquois lived in the area of North America that includes most of central and western New York State. Like the Algonquians, the Iroquois are not a single group of people, but several distinct tribes that speak related languages. These tribes sometimes engaged in warfare with each other. By the early 1600s, the Mohawks, Oneidas, Onondagas, Cayugas, and Senecas joined together to form an **alliance** known as the Iroquois Confederacy. The members of the Iroquois Confederacy had an equal voice in decision making and government. Issues that concerned the entire confederacy were discussed at the Grand Council, a meeting of the chiefs from every tribe. Most issues were discussed at meetings held at the tribal or **clan** level.

Native Americans held councils or meetings to discuss matters of importance to the community and the tribe. For a decision to be made, it was usually necessary for all those in the council to be in agreement.

Government in New Netherland

Reports of a rich fur trade in North America convinced Dutch **merchants** to establish **trading posts** along the Hudson River. In 1614, the Dutch established a trading post near present-day Albany. In 1624, settlements were established on Governor's Island near Manhattan, at Albany, and on the Connecticut and the Delaware Rivers by the Dutch West India Company, which was **chartered** by the Dutch government to oversee American trade.

In 1629, the Dutch West India Company created the patroon system to attract more settlers. Patroons were **investors** who provided funds to settle large tracts of land called patroonships. Patroons were given limited **jurisdiction** over those whom they brought to settle on their lands. All the patroonships failed, except Rensselaerswijck, which survived until 1839.

As more colonists arrived, there were increasing demands for the kind of self-government that existed in the Netherlands. Landdags, or meetings of representatives, formed to act as advisers to the resident directors. Local courts were formed in Beverwijck, New Amsterdam, and Esopus.

Petrus Stuyvesant, known by the English name Peter, was the last director of the Dutch colony of New Netherland. Directors were chosen by the Dutch West India Company and expected to run the colony with the company's best interest in mind.

Government in the Colony of New York

The English took over New Netherland in 1664. They renamed it New York to honor James, the Duke of York and the brother of King Charles II. Under the 1664 Articles of Capitulation, the English allowed Dutch colonists to keep most of the rights they enjoyed under the Dutch **constitution**. In 1665, the Duke of York's Laws were issued to the English communities on Long Island. These laws were gradually expanded throughout the entire **province** of New York.

Under the English, New York was governed by a governor and council **appointed** by the crown. Later an assembly was added, and even later the council was given independent legislative responsibilities. The royal governor was appointed by the king. The governor appointed all the colonial officials who were not directly appointed by the king.

New York's colonial legislature consisted of two houses: the Executive Council and the Assembly. The governor appointed the Executive Council, which served as an Upper House, and whose members advised the governor and passed bills. An Assembly, added later, was the Lower House. Its members were elected by the colony's white male property owners. All bills had to be sent to England for approval by the crown.

Edmund Andros served as the royal governor of New York and New Jersey from 1674 until 1681. As royal governor, Andros was appointed by King James II and was responsible for enforcing the king's laws in the colony. When King James II was overthrown by William of Orange, Andros was captured by colonists and sent back to England.

State Government

When the Declaration of Independence was **ratified** in 1776, the British colonies of North America became states. Although the new United States had a national government, each state had its own government and made its own laws. In early 1777, the first New York State constitution set up the state's government. Albany became the state capital in 1797, and it's still New York's capital today.

The state government in Albany makes laws for the state. It is also in charge of providing public education, health care, and other important services for New York State citizens. The money for these services comes from the different kinds of taxes that New York citizens pay. Like the national government, the state government has three branches or parts: the executive branch, the legislative branch, and the judicial branch. Each branch has a different job to do, and each helps keep the other branches from becoming too powerful. This concept of a division of government was first developed in ancient Greece and Rome.

The Capitol Building in Albany was finished in 1899. It took 32 years to build! The small picture shows New York State's official seal. Two figures representing Liberty and Justice stand on either side of a scene of sailing ships on a blue river. A bright sun shines over green mountains. A bald eagle, representing the United States, sits on top of a globe. The word "Excelsior" on the banner means "Ever Upward."

EXCELSIOR

THE GREAT SEAL OF THE STATE OF NEW YORK

The Executive Branch

The executive branch plans the state budget and makes sure all state laws are carried out. The governor of New York is the head of the executive branch. The governor chooses many of the people who help run the state. Today, New York citizens vote for a new governor every four years. There is no limit on the number of times a person can run for governor.

George Clinton was elected as the first governor of New York. Clinton had been a general in George Washington's army and fought against the British and their Indian allies during the American Revolution. The citizens of New York liked him so much that they elected him as governor seven times. Each term was two years in length.

The executive branch includes many departments. The **attorney general** goes to court and represents New York in state trials. The **treasurer** keeps track of how the state's money is spent. Other department heads are in charge of highway and road safety, the state police, public schools, and public health.

Since 1875, all the governors of New York and their families have lived in the Executive Mansion in Albany. One of New York's most famous governors was Theodore Roosevelt. He served as governor from 1899 to 1900 and went on to become president of the United States in 1901.

Theodore Roosevelt

The Legislative Branch

The legislative branch makes laws for the state. New York State's legislative branch has two houses called the **State Assembly** and the **State Senate**. New York State is divided into assembly districts and senate districts. Each district gets to elect one representative to each house. The Assembly always has 150 members, but the number of members of the Senate changes based on population.

The members of the Assembly and the Senate are elected by the citizens of New York for two-year terms. The Assembly and the Senate vote to make New York State's laws. A law begins as a bill that is introduced in the Senate. The Senate **debates** the bill, and if the bill is approved by the Senate, it is sent to the Assembly. If the bill is approved by the Assembly, it is sent to the governor, who has ten days to sign or **veto** the bill. If the governor doesn't sign or veto the bill in ten days, it becomes a law.

This picture shows members of the New York State Assembly taking part in a meeting in the Capitol Building in Albany. Albany was chosen to be the capital of New York because of its central location. People from all parts of the state can easily get to Albany.

The Judicial Branch

The judicial branch is New York State's court system. It includes all New York State courts. Within the state, there are different kinds of courts. Inferior courts are local courts that operate in cities, towns, and villages in the state. They hear a wide range of court cases, from traffic **violations** to cases involving theft or assault. Trials for serious state crimes are held in the superior courts. The appellate courts hear appeals, or requests to change decisions made by the New York Supreme Court. The highest court in New York State is the Court of Appeals, which can change the decisions made by lower courts.

Each court has a **judge** who is in charge of the courtroom. Judges are elected by the people, and some are appointed by the governor. **Juries** decide the outcome of most trials. Being on a jury is an important way for citizens to be a part of New York's government.

State courts only handle trials that have to do with state laws. They settle disagreements between citizens in the state, decide if someone is guilty of breaking a state law, and decide whether or not state laws follow New York's constitution.

The Court of Appeals is the most powerful court in New York State. People who are unhappy with the decisions made by other New York State courts can ask the Court of Appeals to hear the case again. This picture shows the room where the Court of Appeals meets in the Capitol Building in Albany.

19

Local Government

Every state in the United States has its own government. So does every county, village, city, and town. They govern different things and have to work together.

New York State is divided into counties and municipalities. There are 62 counties in New York State. Counties are responsible for providing law enforcement, public safety, health services, and education for the people who live there. Municipalities are cities, villages, and towns with their own forms of government. They are created by special charters given by the state. Local governments provide almost all the services that their residents require. They also have the power to tax residents.

Some municipalities have separate executive and legislative branches, called **mayors** and **city councils**. Mayors and members of city councils are elected by the people. In some municipalities, the city council fills both roles, and the mayor is a **ceremonial** position. Other local governments may have a city council and a city manager, who is hired by the council and supervises the day-to-day business of the city, town, or village.

HARPER'S WEEKLY.

A
JOURNAL OF CIVILIZATION

VOL. II.—No. 87.] NEW YORK, SATURDAY, AUGUST 28, 1858. [PRICE FIVE CENTS.

THE BURNING OF THE CITY HALL, NEW YORK, AUGUST 18, 1858.

New York City's City Hall was built in 1803. In 1858, some fireworks exploded too close to city hall, and it caught fire. Luckily, only the top part of the building was harmed, and it was quickly rebuilt. The small picture from the front page of *Harper's Weekly* shows the crowds that gathered to see the fire. The color photograph shows how city hall looks today.

Your Role as a Citizen of New York State

A citizen of the United States and New York State has certain rights and freedoms. These rights and freedoms are guaranteed by the United States Constitution, the New York State Constitution, and the laws of the state.

The United States and New York constitutions protect the civil rights of citizens. They both guarantee the freedom of speech and press, and the freedom of religious liberty. Citizens are guaranteed the right to vote and the right to a trial by jury, among other civil rights.

A citizen also has certain responsibilities. Citizens are expected to **obey** the rules and laws where they live, such as rules about traffic safety and public order. Citizens have the responsibility to serve as a member of a jury when called to do so. Voting might be the most important responsibility a citizen has. Citizens vote to elect the men and women who will represent them in local, state, and federal government. Citizens are expected to understand the issues in order to vote responsibly.

Glossary

alliance: An agreement between two or more groups to cooperate for specific purposes.

American Revolution: The war that the American colonists fought from 1775 to 1783 to win independence from England.

appointed: Assigned to a position or office.

attorney general: The chief lawyer of a country or state who represents the government during court cases and serves as a legal adviser.

ceremonial: Without authority, used for public or religious events.

charter: Actions taken by a government to establish a city, colony, or corporation. Also, the document used to do this.

citizens: Members of a state or nation entitled to full civil rights.

city council: The legislative body of a city.

clan: A group of families who claim a common ancestor.

colonies: Regions settled by people from another country who keep their loyalty to their homeland.

constitution: The laws and principles by which a nation is governed.

debates: Engages in an argument or discussion over an issue.

government: A system of ruling a state, country, or community.

investors: People who provide money to a company or enterprise in return for potential profit.

judge: Someone who hears, and often decides, court cases.

juries: Groups of citizens who decide the outcomes of court cases.

jurisdiction: Power, authority, or control over a given region.

mayors: Chief executives of cities and towns.

merchants: People who buy and sell items for profit.

obey: To follow or conform to.

province: A territory governed as a political unit of a country.

ratified: Gave formal approval.

representatives: Individuals who speak on behalf of a larger group of people.

republic: A country that is governed by elected representatives and by an elected leader.

settled: Became a resident of a place; to colonized.

State Assembly: The part of the legislative branch of the state government that must approve a law before it is sent to the governor.

State Senate: The part of the legislative branch of the state government where a law is first introduced.

trading posts: Places where people come to exchange goods.

treasurer: An officer who oversees money.

veto: The power of one branch of government to cancel or reject the decisions or actions of another branch.

violation: The act of doing something that is not allowed by laws or rules.

Index

Primary Source List

Page 5. *Declaration of Independence.* John Trumbull. Oil on canvas. ca. 1786 – 1819. Now kept at the Rotunda of the U.S. Capital, Washington, DC.

Page 15. *Photography of Theodore Roosevelt.* Print. ca. 1900.

Page 21. *The Burning of City Hall, New York.* Wood engraving. Printed by Harper's Weekly. 1858.

Websites

Due to the changing nature of Internet links, The Rosen Publishing Group, Inc. has developed an online list of websites related to the subjects of this book. This site is updated regularly. Please use this link to access the list: **http://www.rcbmlinks.com/nysh/gnys**